TERRIFIC TIMELINES
DINOSAURS

RICHARD FERGUSON
& AUDE VAN RYN

Writer: Isabel Thomas

Laurence King Publishing

Contents

Introduction

Welcome! You're about to meet twenty fascinating dinosaurs, from *Archaeopteryx* to *Tyrannosaurus*. You'll find out what era they come from and what makes each so special. There's a fact file of 'essentials' about every dinosaur, too.

At the end of the book, there's a handy glossary of all the long words and what they mean.

Turn to the inside back cover to find a pocket holding your timeline pieces, with instructions for fitting them together. Opposite the pocket are your pop-out dinosaur figures to complete the timeline.

Triassic

If you could travel back in time 230 million years, you might bump into the very first dinosaurs to live on Earth.

They appeared during the Triassic, a time when the world was much warmer and drier than it is today. All of the world's land was joined together in an enormous continent known as Pangea, surrounded by ocean.

Today, we are used to seeing mammals at the top of food chains, but in the Triassic, the archosaurs or 'ruling reptiles' were boss. They included the first crocodiles, as well as small reptiles that moved quickly on two legs instead of four. Perhaps they were particularly well suited to the hot, dry Triassic climate.

Like their archosaur ancestors, the first dinosaurs were small and two-legged. However, there was a big difference between the two, hidden away in their hipbones (pelvis). They would give rise to the 'terrible reptiles' – meaning dinosaurs – that would rule the world for the

The oldest dinosaurs found so far were fossilized 225 million years ago.

Triassic dinosaurs have only been found in Argentina and Africa. Most of them were lizard-hipped meat-eaters.

Life on Earth flourished in the Triassic. By the end of the period, the first frogs, turtles, mammals, crocodiles and lizards had evolved.

MILLION YEARS AGO (MYA)

260

Triassic Era		
EARLY TRIASSIC 252–245 MYA	MID TRIASSIC 245–228 MYA	LATE TRIASSIC 228–200 MYA

200

150

next 130 million years. Scientists divide dinosaurs into two main groups, based on the shape of their pelvis. They are known as ornithischians (bird-hipped dinosaurs) and saurischians (lizard-hipped dinosaurs). Bird-hipped dinosaurs were quite rare during the Late Triassic. Very few fossils have been found. It was only millions of years later that they developed into giant four-legged herbivores, such as stegosaurs, as well as duck-billed dinosaurs that lived in huge numbers around the world.

The first lizard-hipped dinosaurs were also tiny compared to their descendants, which include *Tyrannosaurus rex*. At the end of the Triassic, dinosaurs definitely didn't rule the world. But that was about to change. Around 200 million years ago, around half of the animals on the planet became extinct. Scientists can't be sure why this happened. Perhaps the climate changed following an asteroid strike, or volcanic eruptions. Many massive mammal-like animals were wiped out, but dinosaurs survived. Suddenly they had less competition for food. The age of the dinosaurs had begun.

100

50

PRESENT DAY

Jurassic

In the early Jurassic, the huge continent of Pangea began to split. The chunks of land that would become North America and Africa drifted apart, and water rushed in to fill the valleys between them. More of the world was wet and tropical.

Only small mammals had survived the mass extinction at the end of the Triassic. Dinosaurs, crocodiles and pterosaurs (flying reptiles) began to take over.

In the early Jurassic, bird-hipped dinosaurs spread to new parts of the world. Many new types appeared, some looking very different from their two-legged ancestors. They included armoured dinosaurs, which walked on four legs and had horns and spikes.

Bird-hipped dinosaurs probably became super-sized because their lizard-hipped predators were also getting bigger! The lizard-hipped dinosaurs can be divided into two groups – the sauropodomorphs and the theropods. Meat-eating theropods had features like today's birds and walked on two legs, leaving their arms free to grasp prey. They had sharp

Bird-hipped dinosaur fossils are found in Jurassic rocks all around the world, and especially in North America and Africa. However, lizard-hipped dinosaurs were most common overall.

Most Jurassic plants were conifers and ferns.

The first birds appeared during this period.

MILLION YEARS AGO (MYA)

260

Jurassic Era

200

EARLY JURASSIC 200–176 MYA

MID JURASSIC 176–161 MYA

LATE JURASSIC 161–146 MYA

150

6

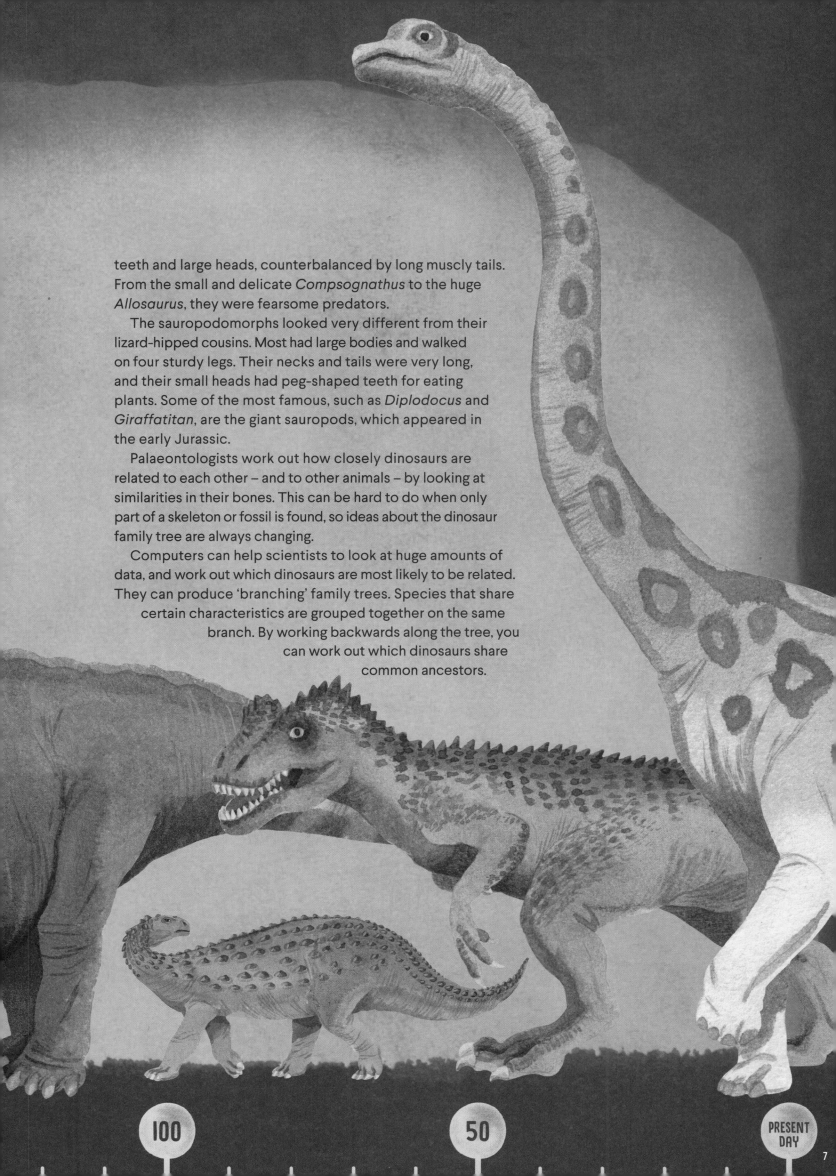

teeth and large heads, counterbalanced by long muscly tails. From the small and delicate *Compsognathus* to the huge *Allosaurus*, they were fearsome predators.

The sauropodomorphs looked very different from their lizard-hipped cousins. Most had large bodies and walked on four sturdy legs. Their necks and tails were very long, and their small heads had peg-shaped teeth for eating plants. Some of the most famous, such as *Diplodocus* and *Giraffatitan*, are the giant sauropods, which appeared in the early Jurassic.

Palaeontologists work out how closely dinosaurs are related to each other – and to other animals – by looking at similarities in their bones. This can be hard to do when only part of a skeleton or fossil is found, so ideas about the dinosaur family tree are always changing.

Computers can help scientists to look at huge amounts of data, and work out which dinosaurs are most likely to be related. They can produce 'branching' family trees. Species that share certain characteristics are grouped together on the same branch. By working backwards along the tree, you can work out which dinosaurs share common ancestors.

100   50   PRESENT DAY

Cretaceous

The Cretaceous period was one of the warmest in the history of our planet. The continents were still moving apart, sea levels had risen and the world was more humid.

The first flowering plants appeared, and became the main type of plant in the world. Parts of the world as far north as France is today were tropical. Even the North and South Poles were no colder than the UK is today.

Bird-hipped herbivores were becoming the most common types of dinosaurs. They were bigger and more varied than ever before, from huge armoured ankylosaurs and horned ceratopsians, to duck-billed hadrosaurs. Not all herbivores were doing as well. There were fewer sauropods than before, perhaps because their main plant food was also becoming less common. However, the sauropods that were left, such as *Argentinosaurus* and *Dreadnoughtus*, became the biggest animals to ever walk the Earth.

Theropods such as *Tyrannosaurus rex* became the ultimate killing machines.

All but a few bird-like dinosaurs were wiped out by a mass extinction event.

Some bird-hipped dinosaurs lived in herds, and had complex social interactions, like today's birds. Others developed tough body armour, spikes and horns.

The other main group of lizard-hipped dinosaurs – the theropods – now included giant predators such as *Tyrannosaurus rex*, and smaller, feathered dinosaurs such as *Velociraptor*.

At the end of the Cretaceous period, another massive extinction wiped out many types of animals, including most of the dinosaurs. Many scientists think that a huge asteroid sent so much dust into the atmosphere that the sun's light was blocked for months. Without light, plants can't make food, and without plants, most dinosaurs would have had nothing to eat. This includes the meat-eaters that ate herbivores! Extinction could also have been caused by climate change, which happens more slowly but can be just as catastrophic.

Dinosaurs did not die out completely. Certain theropods survived, and were the ancestors of today's birds. Each time you spot a pigeon, sparrow or even an ostrich, you are looking at a modern-day dinosaur!

To become fossilized, an animal needs to die where it will be quickly covered up by sand, dust, ash or mud. Not many land animals die like this, so there are many gaps in the fossil record. Scientists have described about 900 different types of dinosaurs, but there are hundreds or thousands more that we don't yet know about.

Cretaceous Era

| MID CRETACEOUS 120–100 MYA | 100 | LATE CRETACEOUS 100–66 MYA | | 50 | | PRESENT DAY |

COELOPHYSIS

In 1947, palaeontologists discovered an amazing Triassic graveyard. Hundreds of *Coelophysis bauri* skeletons had been buried and fossilized in a single place in New Mexico, USA.

The place was Ghost Ranch, a quarry famous for its Triassic fossils. 210 million years ago, this area of the world would have been much closer to the equator, with a tropical climate. Scientists think that a flood caused by heavy rains could have washed a whole flock of these small dinosaurs into a pond, along with fish from the river and other Triassic animals. Covered by muddy water, they died in the perfect conditions to become fossilized eventually. The Ghost Ranch flock included many young *Coelophysis*, with shorter snouts and relatively larger eyes than the adults.

Coelophysis was a small and quick meat-eater and hunted fast-moving insects and small animals. Two of the fossils seem to have a bellyful of tiny crocodilians!

Coelophysis was an early theropod dinosaur, related to the huge meat-eaters of the Jurassic and Cretaceous, such as *Allosaurus* and *Tyrannosaurus*. Some of the features that made these predators so fearsome are found in *Coelophysis* – such as their complex serrated teeth. Each serration is surrounded by microscopic folds, which help to make them extremely strong. All the better for ripping through meat and bones without losing a tooth!

Like today's birds of prey, *Coelophysis* had very sharp eyesight for hunting.

Coelophysis is named after its hollow arm and leg bones, which would have made it very light and fast. Today's birds also have hollow bones.

The fact that so many *Coelophysis* died together at Ghost Ranch is a big clue that they lived in flocks or herds.

COELOPHYSIS ESSENTIALS

MEANING	HOLLOW FORM
TYPE SPECIES	*COELOPHYSIS BAURI*
PERIOD	TRIASSIC
LIVED	210 MYA
DIET	CARNIVORE
FIRST NAMED	1887
ADULT LENGTH	3 METRES
ADULT HEIGHT	1.2 METRES AT THE HIPS
WEIGHT	12.6 KG

DINOSAUR LOCATOR
Dinosaur fossils are actually quite rare at Ghost Ranch. Most of the fossils found belong to other types of ancient reptiles.

LONG TAIL

SHARP EYESIGHT

COELOPHYSIS SKELETONS HAVE A 'WISHBONE' LIKE TODAY'S CHICKENS.

LONG NECK

NIMBLE LEGS

SMALL ARMS

CLAWS

EOCURSOR

By comparing *Eocursor* fossils with those from other dinosaurs, scientists have worked out what the complete skeleton looked like.

The only *Eocursor* skeleton found so far was not fully grown when it died. Scientists may learn more about this very early dinosaur if more fossils are found in the future.

Palaeontologists know very little about the first bird-hipped dinosaurs, because very few fossils have been found. *Eocursor* is one of the most complete.

Fossilized bones from *Eocursor* were first found in 1993, but it was fourteen years until scientists took a close look and named the new dinosaur. Only a quarter of the skeleton has been found, including parts of its skull, jaw, backbone and arms and legs. The bones that have been found are from a fox-sized dinosaur that was not yet fully grown when it died. This means we don't know how big *Eocursor* grew.

Scientists do know that *Eocursor* was a speedy sprinter, thanks to its long legs. Like the bird-hipped dinosaurs that came later, *Eocursor* had teeth suited to eating plants, so it probably used its speed to escape from predators rather than to chase prey. Large hands with grasping fingers are another clue that *Eocursor* was an early bird-hipped dinosaur.

Triceratops, *Pachycephalosaurus*, *Ankylosaurus* and *Stegosaurus* are all bird-hipped dinosaurs too. It's likely that they are related to *Eocursor*, so the fossils from this tiny, two-legged Triassic dinosaur are helping scientists to find out more about how the four-legged giants evolved.

Eocursor has a specially shaped pelvis that sticks out backwards towards the tail – just like a bird's pelvis today. This is what led to the name 'ornithischian' (bird-hipped) dinosaurs.

BIRD-LIKE PELVIS

TRIANGULAR TEETH

LARGE HANDS

LONG LEGS

LONG TAIL

EOCURSOR HAS BEEN NICKNAMED THE 'ROAD RUNNER' DINOSAUR AFTER THE SMALL BUT SPEEDY CARTOON CHARACTER.

EOCURSOR ESSENTIALS

MEANING	LITTLE DAWN RUNNER
TYPE SPECIES	*EOCURSOR PARVUS*
PERIOD	LATE TRIASSIC
LIVED	220 MYA
DIET	HERBIVORE
FIRST NAMED	2007
ADULT LENGTH	I METRE
ADULT HEIGHT	30 CM AT THE HIPS
WEIGHT	2 KG

DINOSAUR LOCATOR
Eocursor fossils have only been found in one place – on a farm in South Africa. A few fossils from Triassic bird-hipped dinosaurs have also been found in Argentina.

EORAPTOR

For a dinosaur not much bigger than a chicken, *Eoraptor* gets a lot of attention. It is one of the oldest two-legged dinosaurs ever discovered.

At first, scientists thought *Eoraptor* was a meat-eating ancestor of *Tyrannosaurus*. It walked on two legs, had short 'arms', and curved claws that look perfect for catching prey. No wonder it was named 'raptor'. But a closer look at *Eoraptor* fossils has revealed clues that it might be more closely related to giant, plant-eating sauropods such as *Diplodocus*.

Some scientists think *Eoraptor* was an ancestor of both theropods and sauropods. As more Triassic fossils are found we may find out exactly where it belongs.

Like most dinosaurs, *Eoraptor* has a mouth packed with more than 100 teeth. They include small, sharp, serrated teeth *and* rounded, leaf-shaped teeth. This shows that it was probably an omnivore, eating soft plants and hunting small prey. *Eoraptor*'s skull has large nostrils, and signs of a keratin beak, like many early sauropodomorphs. Twisted 'finger' bones are another clue that links it to plant-eating dinosaurs. Its long, lean legs would have been good for sprinting – but perhaps they were used not for catching prey, but escaping predators such as *Herrerasaurus*!

Eoraptor may not have been a dinosaur at all, but an archosaur (the ancestors of the dinosaurs)!

EORAPTOR ESSENTIALS

MEANING	EARLY PLUNDERER, DAWN THIEF
TYPE SPECIES	*EORAPTOR LUNENSIS*
PERIOD	TRIASSIC
LIVED	230 TO 225 MYA
DIET	OMNIVORE
FIRST NAMED	1993
ADULT LENGTH	1.2 METRES
ADULT HEIGHT	50 CM
WEIGHT	2 KG

DINOSAUR LOCATOR
Most of what we know about the earliest dinosaurs is based on fossils found in the Ischigualasto Formation in Argentina. 230 million years ago it was covered in swampy forests. Bones had a high chance of being buried in water and sediment, so the area is rich in fossils.

The Ischigualasto Formation is a dry, windy desert. The area is so important for the study of geology that it is a World Heritage Site.

LARGE NOSTRILS

SMALL HEAD

SHORT FORELIMBS

THREE CLAWED 'FINGERS'

LONG BACK LEGS

EORAPTOR'S BONES WERE HOLLOW AND EXTREMELY LIGHT.

HERRERASAURUS

Herrerasaurus lived at the time when the very first dinosaurs evolved. It shows us what the ancestors of all dinosaurs would have looked like.

Herrerasaurus was named after an Argentinian cattle farmer called Victorino Herrera. He was the guide who helped palaeontologists to find *Herrerasaurus* fossils in 1961. Only the back half of the skeleton was discovered, so no one knew exactly what *Herrerasaurus* looked like until new fossils were found in the 1980s. It was like putting together a large *Herrerasaurus*-shaped jigsaw, using pieces from lots of different dinosaurs. Although the jigsaw is complete, scientists aren't yet sure that *Herrerasaurus* is a proper dinosaur. It has most of the features that dinosaurs share, but a few are missing.

Scientists can be certain that *Herrerasaurus* was a fearsome carnivore! It had long fingers that ended in claws for grasping, serrated teeth, and a flexible jaw. Fossils of other plants and animals found near *Herrerasaurus* tell us about its habitat. *Herrerasaurus* lived in tall conifer forests. It would have run through ferns and horsetails to hunt mammal-like reptiles, lizards, amphibians and even huge Triassic insects.

HERRERASAURUS ESSENTIALS

MEANING	HERRERA'S LIZARD
TYPE SPECIES	*HERRERASAURUS ISCHIGUALASTENSIS*
PERIOD	LATE TRIASSIC
LIVED	225 MYA
DIET	CARNIVORE
FIRST NAMED	1963
ADULT LENGTH	3 TO 4 METRES
ADULT HEIGHT	1.1 METRES AT THE HIPS
WEIGHT	180 KG

DINOSAUR LOCATOR
Herrerasaurus fossils are found in the Ischigualasto Formation of northwestern Argentina. It is the only place in the world where scientists can find fossils from every stage of the Triassic.

Horsetails are known as 'living fossils' as they are the only survivors of a plant family that outlived the dinosaurs.

Herrerasaurus fossils were found in 1958, but they were locked up at a port in Argentina for two years, and forgotten!

SLIM NECK

RECTANGULAR SKULL

SHORT ARMS

THREE LONG FINGERS

LONG BACK LEGS

Some scientists think *Herrerasaurus* could be an early type of theropod dinosaur. Others think it may not be a proper dinosaur at all.

HERRERASAURUS HAD A FLEXIBLE JAW TO HELP IT GRIP STRUGGLING PREY WITHOUT GETTING HURT.

MUSSAURUS

Giant, lumbering, ferocious... dinosaurs have been called many things. When *Mussaurus* was discovered, a new word was added to the list: cute.

A tiny skeleton was found in the 1970s. At just 20 cm long, it was no bigger than a rat, and palaeontologists named it 'mouse lizard'. However, there were plenty of clues that this skeleton was just a baby. It was found with six similar skeletons, and two fossilized eggs. But where were the parents? Scientists realized that these baby skeletons, and adults previously thought to be *Plateosaurus*, belonged to a brand new species: *Mussaurus*.

Fossil skulls show that baby *Mussaurus* had a big head, huge eyes and a short, rounded snout, like many baby animals today. Cute looks encourage parents to look after their offspring rather than abandon them or, worse, eat them! The adult *Mussaurus* cared for its babies, protecting them in the nest until they were big enough to fend for themselves.

Mussaurus changed a lot as it grew – no wonder it took so long for scientists to connect the adult skeletons with their big-headed babies. Its skull grew around three times longer, and its eyes narrowed. Its legs became strong and sturdy. Its body grew much faster than its head; *Mussaurus* had a small brain for its body size. Long bones in its front legs suggest that it went around on four legs, using its long neck to reach tasty leaves.

Some scientists think that sauropodomorphs such as *Mussaurus* were the ancestors of giant sauropods including *Apatosaurus*.

Mussaurus probably used its long, rounded teeth to strip needles from pine trees, and nibble at ferns. Young *Mussaurus* may have snacked on small insects too.

SHARP TEETH

LONG NECK

BROAD TAIL (AT THE HIP)

LARGE CLAW (THUMB)

STRONG THIGH BONES

FIVE DIGITS

Fossils from adult, baby and even 'teenage' *Mussaurus* have been found, which show how they changed as they grew.

MUSSAURUS HATCHED FROM EGGS LESS THAN 3 CM LONG.

MUSSAURUS ESSENTIALS

MEANING	MOUSE LIZARD
TYPE SPECIES	*MUSSAURUS PATAGONICUS*
PERIOD	LATE TRIASSIC
LIVED	228 TO 209 MYA
DIET	HERBIVORE
FIRST NAMED	1979
ADULT LENGTH	3 METRES
ADULT HEIGHT	80 CM
WEIGHT	100 KG

DINOSAUR LOCATOR
Mussaurus was discovered in an area of Argentina called Patagonia. The rocks here were formed roughly 215 million years ago, which allows scientists to work out when *Mussaurus* lived.

LONG TAIL

PLATEOSAURUS

Plateosaurus was one of the first dinosaurs to grow really BIG. Its fossils are easy to find for a Triassic dinosaur, so scientists know lots about it.

Peering at bones through a microscope can tell scientists how quickly they grew. It's a bit like counting rings in a tree trunk! *Plateosaurus* bones were surprising – they showed that some adult *Plateosaurus* became huge, while others stopped growing at half the size. *Plateosaurus* may have been able to develop at different rates, depending on the conditions of its environment. Some of today's reptiles use the same trick – but *Plateosaurus* is the only dinosaur shown to do it. Another explanation is that smaller plateosaurs may belong to a different species, or that females were smaller than males (or the other way round).

Plateosaurus' leaf-shaped teeth show that it ate plants. Other Triassic herbivores had to stick to plants that grew near the ground, but standing on its back legs, *Plateosaurus* could stretch out its long neck and nibble trees too. Long, sharp claws would have helped it to grasp and tear branches. Until the giant Jurassic sauropods came along, *Plateosaurus* had this treetop buffet to itself!

Plateosaurus was an early sauropodomorph, which means it is related to giant sauropods such as *Apatosaurus*. By studying *Plateosaurus'* flexible growth, scientists hope to find clues as to how the sauropods grew so enormous.

Some scientists thought that *Plateosaurus* hopped like a kangaroo, but 3D computer modelling shows that it most likely strolled along on two legs.

Plateosaurus engelhardti was named after German scientist Johann Friedrich Engelhardt, who found the first *Plateosaurus* fossils.

SMALL HEAD

LONG NECK

At one German site, bones from at least 50 of these dinosaurs were found in the same place.

STOCKY BODY

LONG BACK LEGS

FIVE FINGERS

FIVE TOES

PLATEOSAURUS FOSSILS ARE OFTEN FOUND TOGETHER, WHICH IS A CLUE THAT THEY LIVED IN HERDS.

PLATEOSAURUS ESSENTIALS

MEANING	FLAT LIZARD, BROAD LIZARD
TYPE SPECIES	*PLATEOSAURUS ENGELHARDTI*
PERIOD	LATE TRIASSIC
LIVED	210 MYA
DIET	HERBIVORE
FIRST NAMED	1837
ADULT LENGTH	6 TO 8 METRES
ADULT HEIGHT	UNKNOWN
WEIGHT	4,000 KG

DINOSAUR LOCATOR
Over 100 *Plateosaurus* fossils have been found, in more than 40 places in Germany, Switzerland and France.

ALLOSAURUS

Allosaurus was one of the biggest, baddest predators of the Late Jurassic. It was powerful enough to take down the giant sauropods that shared its stomping ground.

Allosaurus had a very strong skull, but its bite was a quarter the strength of the bite of a *Tyrannosaurus* and only around half as powerful as the bite of a lion today. Instead of slicing through flesh and bone, *Allosaurus* may have slammed its jaws into prey at high speed, held on with its arms and used strong neck muscles to pull its head back and tear off a chunk of flesh. This is similar to the way a Komodo dragon feeds today. *Allosaurus'* jaws were lined with serrated teeth, between 5 and 10 cm long. They all curved backwards, to help *Allosaurus* keep a good grip on struggling prey.

Allosaurus toothmarks have been found on the fossils of huge dinosaurs, such as *Apatosaurus* and *Stegosaurus*. *Allosaurus* would have scavenged too, looking out for even bigger sauropods that were dead or dying.

Scientists know more about *Allosaurus* than most theropods, because fossils have been found from dinosaurs of many different ages. They show that *Allosaurus* was adult-sized after 15 years, and lived until it was around 25. By contrast, large sauropods could live for 50 years or more.

Allosaurus skeletons are full of clues that their powerful attacks often got them injured – but that they healed well. One skeleton has at least ten different injuries, including broken bones, damaged claws, and infections. Puncture wounds from *Stegosaurus* spikes have been found in the tail and pelvis bones of two different Allosaurs. Teeth broken off during meals would have grown back quickly.

ALLOSAURUS ESSENTIALS

MEANING	DIFFERENT LIZARD
TYPE SPECIES	*ALLOSAURUS FRAGILIS*
PERIOD	LATE JURASSIC
LIVED	150 TO 144 MYA
DIET	CARNIVORE
FIRST NAMED	1877
ADULT LENGTH	12 METRES
ADULT HEIGHT	4.5 METRES AT THE HIPS
WEIGHT	1,500 TO 2,000 KG

DINOSAUR LOCATOR
Most *Allosaurus* fossils were found in western North America – bones from more than 45 different individuals have been found in one Utah quarry alone – and Portugal. Fossils from its descendants have been found in Africa and Australia as well as North America.

Forward-facing eyes allowed *Allosaurus* to judge depth like we can. It would have been good at leaping on prey directly in front of it.

Allosaurus could run at around 20 miles per hour. This is slower than a human sprinter, but fast enough to outrun its plodding prey!

Allosaurus was named after the bones in its back, which looked very different from those of other dinosaurs.

SHORT BONY HORNS

LARGE JAW

THREE FINGERS

THREE TOES

BIG PAWS

HUGE CLAWS (15 CM)

HEAVY FEET

LARGE LEGS

LONG TAIL

ALLOSAURUS' THIGH BONES WERE UP TO A METRE LONG.

ARCHAEOPTERYX

Is it a bird? Is it a plane? Or is it a... dinosaur? When the first *Archaeopteryx* skeleton was found, scientists thought it might be one of the very earliest birds.

This dinosaur is closely related to raptors such as *Sinornithosaurus*. These dinosaurs had stubby or bristly feathers, but couldn't fly. They probably developed feathers for warmth.

For a fossil the size of a raven, *Archaeopteryx* managed to take the world by storm. The reason is the amazing feather prints that surrounded its perfectly preserved bones. Scientists have looked closely at *Archaeopteryx*'s wings and found that they were the right shape for flying or gliding. But having feathered wings is not enough to take to the air. Birds also need brains powerful enough to carry out this complicated task. Brains are made of soft tissue, which cannot become fossilized. Luckily, the brains of birds often leave marks behind on the skull. These marks tell scientists how big different areas of the brain were.

However, *Archaeopteryx* also has several features that living birds don't have – teeth, a long bony tail, special bones to protect its soft belly, and claws at the end of its wings. Interestingly, the large ridge that all birds have on their chests, where the strong flight muscles attach, is also missing.

It's possible that *Archaeopteryx* could flap its wings without ever taking to the skies. Flapping may have been useful for gliding, or keeping balance when holding down prey. The feathers may have been there to keep *Archaeopteryx* warm. All this suggests that *Archaeopteryx* was not the first bird or the ancestor of all birds, but it's still a very important fossil.

Its brain print shows that it had good balance and good eyesight, another clue that it might have been able to fly.

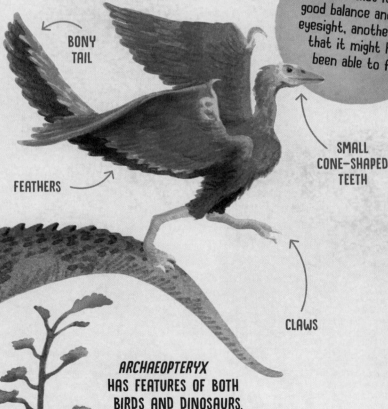

BONY TAIL

FEATHERS

SMALL CONE-SHAPED TEETH

CLAWS

ARCHAEOPTERYX HAS FEATURES OF BOTH BIRDS AND DINOSAURS, AND MAY BE SOMEWHERE BETWEEN THE TWO.

ARCHAEOPTERYX ESSENTIALS

MEANING	ANCIENT WING
TYPE SPECIES	ARCHAEOPTERYX LITHOGRAPHICA
PERIOD	LATE JURASSIC
LIVED	147 MYA
DIET	CARNIVORE
FIRST NAMED	1861
ADULT LENGTH	50 CM
ADULT HEIGHT	70 CM
WEIGHT	500 GRAMS

DINOSAUR LOCATOR
A quarry worker found the first *Archaeopteryx* skeleton in Germany's famous Solnhofen Formation. Today it is the most valuable fossil in the Natural History Museum in London.

DILOPHOSAURUS

You wait ages for a dinosaur... then three come at once! That's what happened in 1942 when the first *Dilophosaurus* fossils were discovered in Arizona, USA.

At first, scientists thought they belonged to another large Jurassic meat-eater, *Megalosaurus*. In 1964, a complete skull was found and scientists realized they were looking at a completely new dinosaur. The big clue was two bony crests on the snout.

Dilophosaurus was one of the first large meat-eating dinosaurs. Because three skeletons were found together, scientists think that it may have hunted in small family groups.

Although *Dilophosaurus* had sharp teeth, it could not kill prey with a deadly bite. Its jaws were too weak. Instead, it used its teeth to pluck meat from carcasses. Does this mean that it was a scavenger, or did it kill animals using its hands and feet?

Scientists have found several clues that *Dilophosaurus* did kill its own food. Its hands have opposable 'thumbs' that let it grasp prey, while the claws on its feet would have made good weapons. One of the *Dilophosauruses* found in Arizona had eight major injuries when it died – a record for any theropod! These included broken and infected bones in its arms and hands that may have been caused when hunting and killing prey.

Dilophosaurus lived near rivers and lakes, and may have hunted fish.

DILOPHOSAURUS ESSENTIALS

MEANING	TWO-CRESTED LIZARD
TYPE SPECIES	*DILOPHOSAURUS WETHERILLI*
PERIOD	EARLY JURASSIC
LIVED	200 TO 190 MYA
DIET	CARNIVORE
FIRST NAMED	1954 / 1970
ADULT LENGTH	6 TO 7 METRES
ADULT HEIGHT	2.4 METRES
WEIGHT	450 KG

DINOSAUR LOCATOR
Dilophosaurus wetherilli skeletons have only been found in Arizona, USA. Fossils from a similar species have been found in China.

Dilophosaurus was one of the first theropods to have bony crests on its snout. They were probably used for display – a bit like the tail of male peacocks – or to help Dilophosauruses recognize each other.

DILOPHOSAURUS WEIGHED ABOUT THE SAME AS A SMALL HORSE.

FAN-SHAPED CRESTS

LARGE HEAD

LARGE TEETH

NOTCHED JAW LIKE A CROCODILE'S

HANDS WITH FIVE DIGITS

DIPLODOCUS

Diplodocus is one of the most famous dinosaurs in the world, yet this super sauropod is still full of surprises.

Diplodocus boasts the longest complete dinosaur skeleton ever found. Its neck stretched more than three times further than a giraffe's neck, and was balanced by an even longer tail! Was this huge neck held straight up to reach tree tops, out in front to 'mow' crops from the ground, or even curved like a flamingo's neck today? To work it out scientists looked at how the neck bones fitted together. Because most of its weight was towards the back of its body, scientists think *Diplodocus* may have been able to sit back on its hind legs to nibble from the tops of trees. It fed on low-growing plants too.

For each tooth *Diplodocus* had five others waiting to take its place, and one tooth was replaced every 35 days. If *Diplodocus* fed on low-lying plants, it may have grabbed mouthfuls of grit by mistake, wearing its teeth down quickly. Fresh teeth every six months would have made them the best tools for chomping soft plants quickly.

Diplodocus and its close relatives had a tail that tapered to a very thin and bendy tip. This is a clue that the tail was used for more than balancing. Computer modelling shows that when *Diplodocus* wriggled its colossal bottom, the momentum transferred to the tail meant that the tip moved faster than the speed of sound! Like a whip, it would have made a cracking or booming sound.

DIPLODOCUS ESSENTIALS

MEANING	DOUBLE BEAM
TYPE SPECIES	*DIPLODOCUS LONGUS*
PERIOD	JURASSIC
LIVED	156 TO 145 MYA
DIET	HERBIVORE
FIRST NAMED	1878
ADULT LENGTH	26 METRES
ADULT HEIGHT	14 METRES
WEIGHT	25,000 KG

DINOSAUR LOCATOR
Diplodocus skeletons have been found in the USA, in an area known as the Morrison Formation (centred in Wyoming and Colorado). One skeleton was up to 33 metres long – the length of three double decker buses.

The enormous tail may have been used to scare off predators or sauropod rivals, or for long-distance communication with other *Diplodocuses*.

PENCIL-SHAPED TEETH

NOSTRILS SET BACK ON HEAD

LONG NECK

BROAD SQUARE SNOUT

ENORMOUS TAPERING TAIL

TINY HEAD

FIVE TOES

DIPLODOCUS WAS SO BIG IT HAD TO EAT CONSTANTLY TO SURVIVE.

LARGE CLAWS

Diplodocus shared its Jurassic habitat with other giant sauropods, such as *Supersaurus* and *Dreadnoughtus*. They may have been longer than *Diplodocus*, but only parts of their skeletons have been found.

GIRAFFATITAN

Imagine being called the wrong name for almost a hundred years! This is how long it took for scientists to realize that *Giraffatitan* was not a *Brachiosaurus*.

Giraffatitan and *Brachiosaurus* are two of the heaviest and tallest sauropod dinosaurs that ever lived. They both have long, giraffe-like necks, front legs longer than their back legs, and relatively short tails compared to *Diplodocus*. No wonder *Giraffatitan* was originally named *Brachiosaurus brancai*.

During the twentieth century, some scientists began to have their doubts. Around a hundred years after 'Brachiosaurus brancai' was first dug up, careful comparison of fossil bones helped confirm that it was actually a completely different animal, just as lions and tigers are different. They renamed it *Giraffatitan*.

Scientists are very interested in the way sauropods' huge bodies worked. None of today's land animals reach this enormous size. Most confusing of all is the extraordinarily long neck. If *Giraffatitan* held its neck out in front, it would have been able to eat a huge amount of food while standing still, saving vital energy. Like giraffes today, it may also have used its neck to nibble very tall plants – but a giraffe doesn't need to grow as a tall as a four-storey building to do this!

Some scientists wonder if long necks helped *Giraffatitan* cool their huge bodies. All large animals risk overheating – elephants solve the problem by using their huge ears to radiate heat away from their bodies. A sauropod's long neck would do a similar job. Imagine a herd of *Giraffatitans* cooling their necks in the breeze!

Although *Giraffatitan* and *Brachiosaurus* skeletons are similar in size, scientists have spotted at least 26 big differences in their fossils that would have made them look very different when they were alive.

BONY CREST

SMALL HEAD

SET BACK NOSTRILS

Giraffatitan had nostrils set back on top of its head, so it didn't have to stop eating to breathe.

VERY LONG NECK

Neck bones have been discovered that hint at even bigger sauropods, including *Argentinosaurus*.

MEDIUM TAIL

WITH NO CHEWING TEETH TO HELP, *GIRAFFATITAN* HAD TO GRAZE ALMOST CONSTANTLY TO CONSUME ENOUGH ENERGY TO POWER ITS HUGE BODY.

LONG FRONT LEGS

GIRAFFATITAN ESSENTIALS

MEANING	GIANT GIRAFFE
TYPE SPECIES	*GIRAFFATITAN BRANCAI*
PERIOD	LATE JURASSIC
LIVED	155 TO 140 MYA
DIET	HERBIVORE
FIRST NAMED	1988
ADULT LENGTH	23 TO 25 METRES
ADULT HEIGHT	13 METRES
WEIGHT	23 TO 25,000 KG

DINOSAUR LOCATOR
The first *Giraffatitan* fossils were found in Tanzania in Africa in the early 1900s, and named as *Brachiosaurus brancai* in 1914.

SCELIDOSAURUS

This small, knobbly plant-eater is pretty important. Scelidosaurus is helping scientists work out why armoured dinosaurs developed such impressive shields.

Scelidosaurus was one of the first armoured dinosaurs. It may be an ancestor of *Ankylosaurus* or *Stegosaurus*, or both. It is much smaller than these Cretaceous giants, but shares the four-legged stance and tough skin studded with bony plates called osteoderms. These looked spongy inside, with an outer layer of tougher bone.

Scelidosaurus was the first complete dinosaur skeleton ever found, and its fossils are some of the best in the world. They are found in limestone, and revealed by soaking the stone in weak acid. Gradually the limestone dissolves, leaving the fossils behind. Even some soft tissue, such as skin, has been fossilized. This is very rare. It showed scientists that the bony plates of *Scelidosaurus* – and probably all armoured dinosaurs – were embedded in the skin. The plates may have been used to deter predators (biting down on *Scelidosaurus* would certainly lead to toothache), or for display. *Scelidosaurus*' beak and leaf-shaped teeth helped it to shred leaves from ferns and conifers. Skull fossils show that *Scelidosaurus* had cheeks, and could probably grab a large mouthful of food at a time. It didn't have grinding teeth, so it probably swallowed stones to help break up food in its stomach, like crocodiles and birds do today.

Scelidosaurus fossils are found on land that would have been underwater in the Early Jurassic. Perhaps a herd or family got washed out to sea during a flood or tsunami, dying in the perfect conditions to become fossilized.

Amazingly, some *Scelidosaurus* skeletons are still articulated, which means the bones are joined together. This makes it easier to work out what the dinosaur looked like.

SCELIDOSAURUS ESSENTIALS

MEANING	LIMB LIZARD
TYPE SPECIES	*SCELIDOSAURUS HARRISONII*
PERIOD	EARLY JURASSIC
LIVED	206 TO 180 MYA
DIET	HERBIVORE
FIRST NAMED	1861
ADULT LENGTH	4 METRES
ADULT HEIGHT	1 METRE
WEIGHT	200 KG

DINOSAUR LOCATOR
Scelidosaurus is known as the Dorset Dinosaur. It has only ever been found in cliffs near Charmouth, in the south of England. It has a similar shape to *Scutellosaurus*, another early armoured dinosaur found in North America.

CHEEKS

BEAK

ROWS OF BONY PLATES

FAIRLY LONG NECK

SCELIDOSAURUS WAS NAMED BY RICHARD OWEN, THE FAMOUS ENGLISH SCIENTIST WHO INVENTED THE WORD 'DINOSAUR' IN 1842.

FOUR STURDY LEGS

HOOF-LIKE CLAWS

STEGOSAURUS

It took less than ten years to work out how *Stegosaurus'* plates were arranged, but more than 100 years to work out what they were used for!

When the first *Stegosaurus* fossil was unearthed, scientists thought its bony plates must have covered its back, like roof tiles. When another fossil was discovered lying on its side, they realized the truth was even stranger. *Stegosaurus'* plates stood straight up, running from neck to tail in two rows. They weren't attached to the skeleton, but held inside the dinosaur's skin.

What were the plates for? Armour to defend against predators; radiators to keep warm or cool down; a colourful array to attract mates? Proudly displayed plates would have been a handy way to tell who was who, because different stegosaurs had plates of different shapes and sizes.

Fossilized tracks help scientists to work out whether dinosaurs lived alone or in groups. Footprints from baby, juvenile and adult *Stegosauruses* have been found together. These dinosaurs didn't live in herds, but perhaps in small groups for safety.

Damaged tips are a clue that *Stegosaurus'* metre-long tail spikes were used for defence. On the end of a short, muscly tail, they could swing hard enough to punch through the tough skin of a hungry carnivore. There are even *Allosaurus* fossils with wounds from a *Stegosaurus* swipe. *Stegosaurus* grew slower than other dinosaurs, so a weapon like this was important for protection.

Most *Stegosaurus* fossil skeletons have lots of missing pieces. One of the most complete skeletons was discovered by a farmer in a bulldozer! It is now in the Natural History Museum, London.

Stegosaurus is the largest of the stegosaurs, herbivores that roamed Earth from the mid-Jurassic to the early Cretaceous. All stegosaurs had two rows of plates or spines stretching from neck to tail.

Stegosaurus' brain was around the size of a golf ball. Today's largest land animal, the African elephant, has a brain three times larger than a human brain.

STEGOSAURUS ESSENTIALS

MEANING	ROOFED LIZARD
TYPE SPECIES	*STEGOSAURUS STENOPS*
PERIOD	JURASSIC
LIVED	156 TO 144 MYA
DIET	HERBIVORE
FIRST NAMED	1877
ADULT LENGTH	9 METRES
ADULT HEIGHT	4 METRES
WEIGHT	3,500 KG

DINOSAUR LOCATOR
Stegosaur fossils have been found on every continent except Australia and Antarctica. Most *Stegosaurus stenops* fossils have been found in western North America.

18 TO 20 BONY PLATES IN TWO ROWS

BROAD HIPS

SMALL POINTED HEAD

FOUR SPIKES (1 METRE)

THREE BLUNT TOES ON HIND LEGS

This vegetarian probably ate low-growing bushes and plants such as ferns, mosses and cycads. Its beak could be used to crop plants, but it would only have been able to chew soft branches.

FOR A HUGE DINOSAUR, *STEGOSAURUS* HAD TINY TEETH.

FIVE TOES ON FRONT LEGS

ANKYLOSAURUS

As meat-eating dinosaurs got bigger, herbivores had to toughen up. *Ankylosaurus* adapted by developing the best body armour of any dinosaur.

The armour was made of bony plates that grew inside the skin. Today's crocodiles have these plates – called osteoderms – but they are nothing compared to the plates, knobs and spikes that covered *Ankylosaurus*. Even its eyelids contained a thin sheet of bone.

Large plates covered the dinosaur's shoulder and neck area, shielding the most important parts of the body from the huge bite of a *Tyrannosaurus*. Plates along the top and sides of the body were smaller, so *Ankylosaurus* could move freely. To get a bite, a predator would have had to flip *Ankylosaurus* over. This was no easy task because *Ankylosaurus'* body was as wide as a car, and low to the ground. Army tanks are built to the same design!

Although the plates were just a few millimetres thick, they would have been super strong. Each plate was made of lightweight, spongy bone, with a thin coating of bone and strengthened with collagen fibres.

Ankylosaurs are one of two big groups of armoured dinosaurs. They are closely related to other four-legged armoured dinosaurs, such as stegosaurs. *Ankylosaurus* is the biggest ankylosaur found so far.

A large part of *Ankylosaurus'* brain was devoted to smelling. This could have helped them to find food, or avoid predators.

HORNS

WIDE SKULL

BEAK

SPIKES

HEAVY TAIL CLUB

This made the armour light, but tough enough to stand up to a predator's teeth. At the end of *Ankylosaurus'* tail, several plates were fused to a long 'handle' made of tail bones to make a gigantic club. This could be swung from side to side. Scientists have worked out that the largest tail clubs were powerful enough to crush bones and topple giant predators.

They were probably also used to fight or warn off other *Ankylosauruses* in a fearsome display!

The plates had a network of large, pipe-like blood vessels. Scientists have suggested that they may have helped to cool *Ankylosaurus* down.

ANKYLOSAURUS ESSENTIALS

MEANING	STIFF LIZARD, FUSED LIZARD
TYPE SPECIES	*ANKYLOSAURUS MAGNIVENTRIS*
PERIOD	LATE CRETACEOUS
LIVED	67 TO 65 MYA
DIET	HERBIVORE
FIRST NAMED	1908
ADULT LENGTH	6 TO 7 METRES
ADULT HEIGHT	1.7 METRES
WEIGHT	4,000 KG

DINOSAUR LOCATOR
Ankylosaurus fossils have been found in Alberta, Canada and Montana and Wyoming in the USA.

THE WHOLE TAIL CLUB (HANDLE PLUS KNOB) WAS AROUND A METRE LONG.

DEINONYCHUS

Deinonychus was a speedy predator, which is a clue that dinosaurs were warm-blooded like birds, not cold-blooded like crocodiles, which can't run as fast as a bird flies.

Say hello to a very important dinosaur. *Deinonychus* fossils showed that dinos were not lumbering lizards, but could be fast and bird-like.

The first thing you notice about *Deinonychus* is the large, hooked killing claw on one toe of each foot. And back in the Cretaceous it might have been the last thing you noticed, too! We know that *Deinonychus* held its longest claws off the ground as it walked, keeping them super sharp. At first, scientists thought the claw was used for slashing prey, or climbing up gigantic dinosaurs during an attack. Recently, a more gruesome theory has been put forward. Scientists have argued that the claw would have been used like birds of prey use their talons – to hold down struggling prey as they ate it alive! These grasping feet may have eventually helped dinosaurs to climb trees and perch on branches, as they evolved into today's birds.

Deinonychus fossils have been found near fossils of a larger dinosaur called *Tenontosaurus*. There are *Deinonychus* bite marks on the *Tenontosaurus* bones, and even broken *Deinonychus* teeth lying nearby. The teeth probably broke off as *Deinonychus* tried to chomp through the larger dinosaur's ribs. Some of the bite marks are very deep, suggesting that *Deinonychus* had a bite as powerful as a lion or tiger's.

Deinonychus is related to other meat-eating theropod dinosaurs, such as *Troodon* and *Tyrannosaurus*. This group of dinosaurs are distant relations of the birds that you see flying around today.

FEATHERS

SHARP EYESIGHT

STIFF TAIL

TWO LEGS

KILLING CLAW

THERE IS LITTLE DOUBT THAT *TENONTOSAURUS* WAS ONE OF *DEINONYCHUS'* FAVOURITE FOODS!

DEINONYCHUS ESSENTIALS

MEANING	TERRIBLE CLAW
TYPE SPECIES	*DEINONYCHUS ANTIRRHOPUS*
PERIOD	CRETACEOUS
LIVED	120 TO 110 MYA
DIET	CARNIVORE
FIRST NAMED	1969
ADULT LENGTH	3 METRES
ADULT HEIGHT	90 CM AT THE HIPS
WEIGHT	75 KG

DINOSAUR LOCATOR
Several *Deinonychus* skeletons have been found in Montana, USA, including one less than two years old. It looked quite different from adult *Deinonychus*, and may have been able to flap 'wings' like today's birds.

PACHYCEPHALOSAURUS

Pachycephalosaurus is famous for its 'crash helmet' head. Some scientists think these bony domes must have been used for head-butting.

The bony dome on *Pachycephalosaurus'* head is up to 23 cm thick. It has attracted lots of attention because no other animal – dead or alive – has a similar skull. It's hard to deduce dinosaur behaviour from bones, but one theory is that it was used in head-butting competitions to show who was boss, like today's goats do. Scans of fossil domes show dents and damage possibly caused in combat.

Other scientists think that *Pachycephalosaurus'* long neck would not have been strong enough for head-to-head battle. Maybe they butted each other in the body instead, or perhaps the domes were just for showing off. We know that *Pachycephalosaurus* spent time together in herds. Dome size may have been an important sign of a dinosaur's age and status. The rest of the head and snout is covered with small bony spikes and hornlets, which may have added to the display.

In 2016, three skull bones from a tiny *Pachycephalosaurus* were found. Some of its distinctive spikes were already in place. Some scientists think that two types of smaller dinosaurs with spiky skulls – *Dracorex hogwartsia* and *Stygimoloch spinifer* – are actually young *Pachycephalosaurus wyomingensis* yet to grow an adult dome.

No one can be sure what *Pachycephalosaurus'* body looked like, because only skulls have been found. Scientists have made a best guess based on closely related dinosaurs.

PACHYCEPHALOSAURUS ESSENTIALS

MEANING	THICK-HEADED LIZARD
TYPE SPECIES	*PACHYCEPHALOSAURUS WYOMINGENSIS*
PERIOD	CRETACEOUS
LIVED	68 TO 66 MYA
DIET	HERBIVORE OR OMNIVORE
FIRST NAMED	1943
ADULT LENGTH	4.5 METRES
ADULT HEIGHT	3 METRES
WEIGHT	1,000 KG

DINOSAUR LOCATOR
Pachycephalosaurus fossils have been found in several places in North America.

BONY KNOBS

LARGE, SMOOTH DOME

BEAK

Pachycephalosaurus belongs to a family of dinosaurs known as 'boneheads', with thick bony skulls instead of horns. It was the biggest bonehead, and the last before the dinosaurs became extinct.

SMALL ARMS AND HANDS

STRONG LEGS

DRACOREX HOGWARTSIA WAS NAMED 'DRAGON KING OF HOGWARTS' AFTER THE SCHOOL IN THE HARRY POTTER BOOKS.

PARASAUROLOPHUS

Why would a dinosaur need a 180-cm long crest on its head? Since *Parasaurolophus* was discovered almost 100 years ago, there have been many ideas.

Parasaurolophus' crest is made of bone, but it's not solid. A pair of tubes run from the dinosaur's nostrils up to the top of the crest, then loop back down to the throat. Air blown through the tubes would have travelled a total distance of 2.5 metres! Suggested functions include a snorkel to store air while *Parasaurolophus* fed underwater, a system to boost the dinosaur's sense of smell, and a decoration to display while trying to attract a mate.

Computer modelling has allowed scientists to try out another idea – that the crest could be used like a wind instrument to make sounds. The tubes could have worked in the same way as musical instruments. The size and shape of the tubes mean that adults may have made low-pitched sounds as today's whales do, while younger dinosaurs would have sounded more like they were tweeting. Models are a useful way for scientists to test ideas about extinct animals. They have been used to study chewing, bite force, flight, and movement.

So why might dinosaurs need a special sound system? *Parasaurolophus* was very brainy for a dinosaur, and lived together in large herds. Parents and children probably 'talked' to each other a lot. Sounds would also have been useful to warn a herd of danger, or to attract mates. They had very good eyesight, and may have used crests to recognize one another, too.

Parasaurolophus is a hadrosaur, and related to earlier bird-hipped dinosaurs such as *Iguanodon* and *Heterodontosaurus*.

One of the youngest *Parasaurolophus* skulls ever found was discovered by a teenager doing school work.

The crest is divided in half by a septum, just like your nose!

PARASAUROLOPHUS ESSENTIALS

MEANING	LIKE *SAUROLOPHUS*
TYPE SPECIES	*PARASAUROLOPHUS WALKERI*
PERIOD	LATE CRETACEOUS
LIVED	76 TO 74 MYA
DIET	HERBIVORE
FIRST NAMED	1922
ADULT LENGTH	11 METRES
ADULT HEIGHT	4 METRES
WEIGHT	3,500 KG

DINOSAUR LOCATOR
Parasaurolophus lived across a wide area in the part of the world now known as North America.

GRINDING TEETH

BEAK

LARGE BONY CREST

THE FOSSIL OF A BABY *PARASAUROLOPHUS* WAS FOUND IN 2013. IT WAS LESS THAN A YEAR OLD, BUT AS LONG AS A SMALL CAR! A SMALL BUMP ON ITS HEAD SHOWED ITS CREST BEGAN TO GROW FROM BIRTH.

TRICERATOPS

The largest *Triceratops* skull fossil is 2.5 metres long – around the length of a surfboard.

When the first *Triceratops* fossil was unearthed, scientists thought the metre-long eyebrow horns must belong to a gigantic bison fossil. In fact, they had discovered horned dinosaurs!

This bulky beast was one of the largest horned dinosaurs – around the size of an African elephant. Scientists think *Triceratops* probably stood like an elephant too, on strong, stout legs. But what were those huge horns used for? They look handy for self-defence – the perfect height for jabbing a tyrannosaur in the belly. At least one *Triceratops* horn has been found with *Tyrannosaurus* bite marks. But it's likely that the horns became so large because *Triceratops* liked to fight each other.

Many animals lock horns in battle to take control of a territory or attract mates. Sometimes they don't even have to fight – huge horns work like an advert saying 'don't mess with me!' Scientists think that *Triceratops*' extreme horns and frill may have been mainly for display, to impress other *Triceratops*.

Although most *Triceratops* fossils are found alone, three young *Triceratops* were found together in 2005. Young dinosaurs may have stuck together for protection, preferring to live alone as they grew older.

Triceratops' huge frill looks like armour, but it wasn't that tough. Frill fossils have been found with puncture wounds and even tyrannosaur bite marks. It would have been covered in keratin, just like the outer layer of a bird's beak. It may have been as colourful as the bill of a toucan!

Triceratops had amazing teeth that could chomp tough plants without wearing down quickly. Pointy tips worked together like scissors to slice without using much effort. Another part of the tooth was used for chewing. This trick probably helped *Triceratops* to eat a wider range of plants than other herbivores.

TRICERATOPS ESSENTIALS

MEANING	THREE-HORNED FACE
TYPE SPECIES	*TRICERATOPS HORRIDUS*
PERIOD	CRETACEOUS
LIVED	67 TO 65 MYA
DIET	HERBIVORE
FIRST NAMED	1889
ADULT LENGTH	9 METRES
ADULT HEIGHT	4 METRES (AT THE HIPS)
WEIGHT	7,000 KG

DINOSAUR LOCATOR
Triceratops is the most common type of dinosaur unearthed in western North America. More than 50 fossil skulls have been found in Montana's Hell Creek Formation.

Horned dinosaurs are known as ceratopsians. There are more than 30 different types, including *Triceratops*, *Pentaceratops*, *Titanoceratops* and *Torosaurus*. Each type has a different number of horns and spikes. These differences may have helped ceratopsians to recognize their own kind.

Some *Triceratops* frill fossils have holes made by the horns of other *Triceratops*.

EYEBROW HORNS

MASSIVE BONY FRILL WITH UP TO 26 SMALL SPIKES

NOSE HORN

GIGANTIC SKULL

SHORT TAIL

STOUT LEGS

HOOVES

THE OLDER THE *TRICERATOPS*, THE LONGER AND MORE TWISTED THE HORNS.

TROODON

Troodon is a mean-looking meat eater with terrifying teeth, but it had a softer side. Scientists have found clues that *Troodon* was a great parent.

Like today's birds and reptiles, all dinosaurs laid eggs. Scientists are interested in whether dinosaurs looked after their eggs carefully, like most birds, or buried and abandoned them, like most reptiles.

Large batches of *Troodon* eggs have been found, giving scientists a close look at the shells – and even the unhatched baby dinosaurs inside. *Troodon* eggs are wider at the bottom than the top, like birds' eggs. The shells are also very similar to birds' eggs. They show that *Troodon* probably laid the eggs in sand or mud, then sat on top of the 'nest' to keep the eggs warm.

Sometimes adult *Troodon* are found near a fossilized nest. None of them have the special type of bone that female dinosaurs (and birds) develop when they are laying eggs, so there is a good chance that they are males. Scientists think that *Troodon* fathers may have been responsible for looking after the eggs, while mothers hunted for food to stay strong for egg laying. Many birds – but very few reptiles – do this today. Similarities between *Troodon* and birds are exciting, because they help to show that there are close links between meat-eating dinosaurs and today's birds.

Troodon belongs to a family of meat-eaters called the Maniraptora, the dinosaurs thought to be most closely related to today's birds.

Troodon nests contained up to 30 eggs. They were probably laid in pairs, rather than all at once.

LARGE FORWARD-FACING EYES

THREE FINGERS

This dinosaur was named after its sharp, serrated teeth, which curved backwards to deliver a killer bite.

LONG BACK LEGS

CURVED CLAWS

NO OTHER DINOSAUR HAD A LARGER BRAIN FOR ITS BODY SIZE. *TROODON* MAY HAVE BEEN AS CLEVER AS TODAY'S BIRDS.

ONE DINOSAUR HAD A LUCKY ESCAPE – SCIENTISTS FOUND A *TYRANNOSAURUS* TOOTH LODGED INSIDE A HADROSAUR'S TAIL BONE.

TROODON ESSENTIALS

MEANING	WOUNDING TOOTH
TYPE SPECIES	*TROODON FORMOSUS*
PERIOD	LATE CRETACEOUS
LIVED	74 TO 65 MYA
DIET	CARNIVORE
FIRST NAMED	1856
ADULT LENGTH	2.4 METRES
ADULT HEIGHT	90 CM AT THE HIPS
WEIGHT	40 TO 50 KG

DINOSAUR LOCATOR

Troodon has been found as far north as Alaska in the USA. Its large eyes would have helped it to hunt in low light during the short winter days, and perhaps even at night. Bigger teeth show that Alaskan *Troodon* grew up to twice as big as southern *Troodon*, so they must have been very successful predators.

TYRANNOSAURUS

'Sue', 'Big Mike' and 'Stan' don't sound terribly scary ... but they are nicknames for some of the world's most fearsome fossils.

Tyrannosaurus had a large brain for a dinosaur, and may have been clever enough to team up to catch massive prey. However, some scientists think they were too bad-tempered to work as a team. Bite marks on *Tyrannosaurus* fossils show that they got into fights!

Tyrannosaurus walked on its back legs. Huge leg and tail muscles balanced the weight of its massive head. However, *Tyrannosaurus* was probably too large to run. Scientists think it speed-walked at up to 10 miles per hour. The barrel-sized skull is full of clues that *Tyrannosaurus* could hear prey from a great distance and track animals by their smell. Forward-facing eyes (like ours) helped them to grab prey.

The bigger the bite, the bigger the prey. *Tyrannosaurus'* jaws opened more than 65 degrees, allowing it to bite off a lion-sized chunk, with bones, in one go. Bones have been found in *Tyrannosaurus* coprolites (fossilized dung). This dinosaur wasn't fussy. It also scavenged for dead animals, and would have been good at chasing off other diners.

The biggest, most complete *Tyrannosaurus* skeleton was nicknamed Sue after the palaeontologist who dug it up. Scientists can't yet tell if Sue is a male or a female tyrannosaur.

Tyrannosaurus rex's banana-sized teeth were pointed and had saw-like edges for extra cutting power.

LARGE, HOLLOW HEAD

60 TEETH

1.5 METRE SKULL

SMALL ARMS

TWO-FINGERED HANDS

HUGE LEG MUSCLES

TYRANNOSAURUS ESSENTIALS

MEANING	TYRANT LIZARD
TYPE SPECIES	*TYRANNOSAURUS REX*
PERIOD	CRETACEOUS
LIVED	67 TO 65 MYA
DIET	CARNIVORE
FIRST NAMED	1905
ADULT LENGTH	13 METRES
ADULT HEIGHT	4 METRES (AT THE HIPS)
WEIGHT	8,000 KG

DINOSAUR LOCATOR
Sue, Big Mike and Stan were all unearthed in the USA, in a dry, rocky, river valley known as Hell Creek. This is one of the best places in the world to look for dinosaur fossils. Digging through the layers of rock is like time-travelling 65 million years into the past, when the area was leafy, warm and wet.

Glossary

AMPHIBIANS cold-blooded animals that include frogs, toads and newts

ANKYLOSAURS a group of four-legged, armoured dinosaurs

ARCHOSAURS reptiles that were the ancestors of the dinosaurs

ARMOURED DINOSAURS dinosaurs with bony plates along their back, such as ankylosaurs

ASTEROID small rocky object that orbits the Sun and, very rarely, may crash into a planet in an asteroid strike

BIRDS OF PREY birds that hunt other birds and animals for food

BISON a shaggy wild ox with a humped back, which lives in North America and Europe

CARNIVORES animals that eat other animals

CERATOPSIANS horned dinosaurs

COLLAGEN the main material that makes up skin

CONIFER a tree that produces cones, and often has needle-shaped leaves

COPROLITE a piece of fossilized dung

CROCODILIANS large reptiles that include crocodiles, alligators and caimans

CYCAD a tropical plant that looks like a palm tree, but produces cones

DATA facts and statistics about a topic

EQUATOR an imaginary line that divides the Earth into two hemispheres

EXTINCT no longer alive

FOSSILIZED has been preserved as a fossil

GEOLOGY the science of studying Earth's rocks and fossils

HADROSAURS plant-eating dinosaurs, also known as duck-billed dinosaurs for their flattened snouts

HERBIVORES animals that eat plants

HUMID when there is lots of water vapour in the air

JUVENILE a young animal that is not yet fully grown

KERATIN the material from which hair, claws, beaks and feathers are made

KOMODO DRAGON the world's largest living lizard

LIZARD a cold-blooded reptile with four legs, rough scaly skin and a tail

MAMMAL a warm-blooded animal with hair or fur

MYA short for 'million years ago'

NORTHERN HEMISPHERE the half of Earth that lives north of the equator

OMNIVORES animals that eat both plants and animals

ORNITHISCHIANS bird-hipped dinosaurs, including stegosaurs and ankylosaurs

OSTEODERMS bony plates that grow inside the skin

PALAEONTOLOGIST a scientist who studies fossils

PANGEA a huge 'supercontinent' made up of all of Earth's land, which existed millions of years ago

PREDATOR an animal that hunts other animals for food

PTEROSAURS flying reptiles that lived in the Jurassic and Cretaceous periods

RAPTORS meat-eating dinosaurs that walked on two legs and had a large claw on each foot

REPTILES animals with dry, scaly skin, including snakes, lizards, crocodiles and turtles

SAURISCHIANS lizard-hipped dinosaurs

SAUROPODOMORPHS medium-sized plant-eating dinosaurs that lived during the Triassic and early Jurassic periods and were ancestors of the sauropods

SAUROPODS very large plant-eating dinosaurs that walked on four legs, and had a long neck and tail

SEPTUM a piece of tissue that divides two spaces in the body, such as the nostrils

SERRATED jagged

STAGNANT a pool of water that is not flowing

STEGOSAURS plant-eating dinosaurs that include *Stegosaurus*

THEROPODS two-legged meat-eating dinosaurs thought to be very closely related to modern birds

TROPICAL from or in the tropics, the areas of the planet closest to the equator

TSUNAMI a giant sea wave caused by a disturbance such as an earthquake

TYRANNOSAURS giant meat-eating dinosaurs that lived in the late Cretaceous period

WIND INSTRUMENT a musical instrument that makes a sound when you blow into or through it

Published in 2018 by
Laurence King Publishing
361–373 City Road
London EC1V 1LR
United Kingdom
T +44 20 7841 6900
enquiries@laurenceking.com
www.laurenceking.com

Concept © 2018 Richard Ferguson
Illustrations © 2018 Aude van Ryn

This book was produced by Laurence King
Publishing Ltd, London.

A catalogue record for this book is available
from the British Library.

ISBN: 978-1-78627-117-4

Designed by Claire Clewley

Printed in Malaysia